TENNESSEE

impression

FARCOUNTRY
PRESS

photography by **Bob Schatz**

Right: Cypress trees encircle the shores of Reelfoot Lake in northwest Tennessee.

Below: Morning dew hints at Smoky Mountain beauty in the historic town of Pigeon Forge.

Title page: Deer are often sighted in the fields of Cades Cove in Great Smoky Mountains National Park.

Cover: A mare and foals enjoy a quiet morning on a Williamson County farm. Tennessee has a long history of fine horses, first in the early 1800s as a leader in horse racing world, then as the home of the famed Tennessee Walking Horse breed.

Back cover: A purple iris blooms wild in a Tennessee meadow. The cultivated purple iris is commonly accepted as the state's official flower.

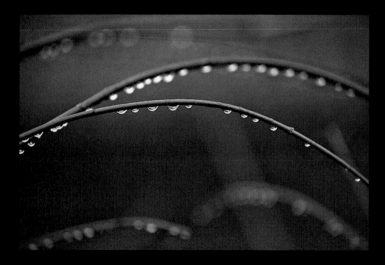

ISBN 10: 1-56037-426-8
ISBN 13: 978-1-56037-426-8

© 2008 by Farcountry Press
Photography © 2008 by Bob Schatz

For more information about our books, write Farcountry Press, P.O. Box 5630, Helena, MT 59604; call (800) 821-3874; or visit www.farcountrypress.com.

Created, produced, and designed in the United States.
Printed in China.

Right, top and bottom: The Tennessee Aquarium in Chattanooga offers glimpses of turtles and other inhabitants of delta waters.

Facing page: The main waterfall at Fall Hollow offers repose along the Natchez Trace Parkway. The parkway is a National Scenic Byway commemorating an ancient trail from the Mississippi River through Alabama to central Tennessee. Travelers may drive, hike, bike, or camp along its 444 miles.

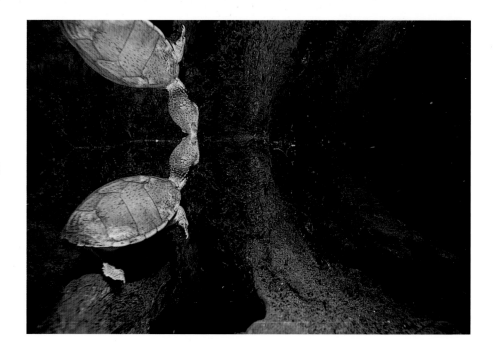

Right: The Nashville skyline rises along the banks of the Cumberland River. Settled in 1779, the city was famous in the nineteenth century for political figures such as Sam Houston and Andrew Jackson. Today, its name is synonymous with American country music.

Below: Ducks make themselves at home in the lobby of the Peabody Hotel in downtown Memphis, where twice daily they take part in the March of the Peabody Ducks. Built in 1925 in the Italian Renaissance style and recently renovated, the hotel is considered one of the South's grandest.

Right: An autumn rainbow brightens the mountaintops of Great Smoky Mountains National Park. The popular park straddles the border between North Carolina and Tennessee.

Below: Lush vegetation covers the rocky backbone of the Chimney Tops formation in Great Smoky Mountains National Park. The Great Smoky Mountains are a small part of the Appalachian Mountains stretching from Maine to Georgia, one of the oldest mountain ranges in the world.

Below left: Fountains on the grounds of Bicentennial Capitol Mall State Park in Nashville attract visitors looking for a break from the heat. The 19-acre park contains 31 fountains, each representing one of Tennessee's predominant waterways. Built to celebrate the state's bicentennial, the park extends out from the grounds of the State Capitol and offers outdoor lessons in history, geography, and civics.

Below right: Children play at the American Museum of Science and Energy in Oak Ridge.

The Belle Meade Mansion, with its limestone columns, is the centerpiece of the Belle Meade Plantation, a 30-acre historic site six miles west of Nashville. Meaning "beautiful meadow," the planta- tion was famous for breeding racehorses, and welcomed President Grover Cleveland in 1884. The mansion was restored to its 1880s appearance and offers educational programs and tours year-round.

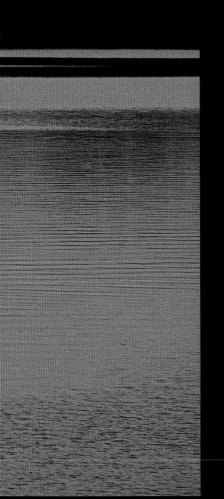

Left: Anglers start fishing at dawn on J. Percy Priest Reservoir, one of the many lakes surrounding Nashville. Formed by a dam on the Stones River, the lake is home to smallmouth and largemouth bass, as well as rockfish, catfish, and more.

Below: The Master of Foxhounds gathers his riders and hounds for a hunt led by central Tennessee's Hillsboro Hounds.

Right, top: Sunflowers are an annual delight at Agricenter International, a nonprofit working farm and educational facility located on the grounds of Shelby Farms Park in Germantown, outside Memphis. The 4,500-acres Shelby Farms Park is the largest urban park in the United States.

Right, bottom: A youngster takes time to admire the base of Daffodil Hill at the Memphis Botanic Garden. The Japanese Garden of Tranquility and the Sensory Garden may be found among its 96 acres of display gardens and woodlands.

Far right: Brilliant fall colors enliven the town of Vonore in far eastern Tennessee's Monroe County.

Red and butter-yellow distinguish this turreted Victorian home in Nashville's historic Edgefield district. Nashville is the oldest permanent settlement in middle Tennessee. It was designated the state capital in 1843.

The Woodruff-Fontaine House Museum on Adams Avenue in Memphis was acquired in 1962 by the Association for the Preservation of Tennessee Antiquities, and restored. A French Victorian mansion built in 1870 along the city's "Millionaire's Row," its grounds include a carriage house and well-established magnolia trees.

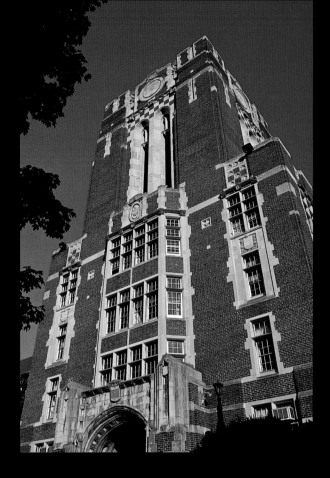

Historic buildings are carefully preserved along Main Street in Jonesborough, which was founded in 1779. Andrew Jackson opened his law practice here and later became a judge. Beginning in 1820, local Quakers and a Main Street print shop produced *The Emancipator*, the nation's first regular periodical devoted to the abolition of slavery.

Built in 1919, Ayres Hall graces the campus of the University of Tennessee, home of the Tennessee Volunteers, in Knoxville. The university began as Blount College in downtown Knoxville in 1794 and later moved to its present location overlooking the Tennessee River.

Above: A spider web, woven amid abundant foliage near Ocoee in southern Tennessee. The nearby Ocoee River boasts some of the finest whitewater rafting opportunities in the southeastern United States.

Right: Fog, a regular visitor in the moist Great Smoky Mountains, shrouds a hiker taking a mountaintop stroll.

Left: Nashville's Public Square and Founders Building commemorate the city's bicentennial.

Below, left: The River Gallery Sculpture Garden is nestled among the distinctive shops and restaurants of Chattanooga's Bluff View Art District, which is named for the 80-foot limestone bluff that sits above the Tennessee River.

Below, middle: Alex Haley Heritage Square, in east Knoxville, features a bronze statue of the award-winning author of *Roots*. Haley spent summers in Henning, Tennessee, where his grandparents introduced him to stories of his ancestors.

Below, right: Man in a Row Boat by sculptor David Phelps is placed in front of the Centre Square II Building in downtown Knoxville and depicts the fisherman and his boat rising out of the water.

Above: LP Field, on the east bank of the Cumberland River in Nashville, is home turf for the Tennessee Titans of the National Football League.

Left: A trusty canoe stands at the ready next to one of Tennessee's approximately 200,000 lakes and ponds.

Left: Tobacco cures in the air of a Tennessee barn. Tobacco is grown in 66 of Tennessee's 95 counties, and competes with cotton and soybeans for status as the state's number one cash crop.

Bottom left: Fresh-from-the-orchard apples are gathered for sale at a farmer's market. Though business of farming has generally replaced farming as a way of life, Tennesseans continue to take pride in what their farms can produce.

Bottom right: What's for dinner? These farmers' market crates display some of the wide variety of fruits and vegetables still grown on Tennessee farms. By the mid-1800s Tennessee's agricultural economy was well-established, and its surplus fed people outside the state and abroad.

Left: Geese fly above the Tennessee River near Loudon. The Tennessee begins at the confluence of the Holston and French Broad rivers in Knoxville, and flows into the Ohio River at Paducah, Kentucky. A 1755 British map shows it as "The River of the Cherakees."

Below: Grass sets seed along the banks of the Tennessee River. In its first ten years, the Tennessee Valley Authority built nine hydroelectric dams along the Tennessee River system. Today the river is the focus of recreation, commerce, and industry.

The Memphis skyline is dramatic as the city eases into night. Memphis has had its economic ups and down historically, but its location on the Mississippi River's east bank helped it become a major distribution center dominant in cotton marketing and hardwood lumber trading. Today, manufacturing, banking and finance dominate Memphis economy.

Right, top and bottom: Visiting fans adorn the rock walls around Graceland with graffiti, or homages to "the King." Born in Tupelo, Mississippi, Elvis Presley moved with his parents to Memphis, where he graduated from Humes High School in 1953. The rhythm and blues music that the teenaged Elvis heard along Beale Street shaped the music that he eventually recorded at the legendary Sun Records.

Facing page: The Graceland Mansion, famous as the one place entertainer Elvis Presley really felt at home, attracts visitors from around the world and offers audio tours in a number of languages. Presley and members of his family are buried in the Meditation Garden on the 14-acre grounds.

Right: Cattle graze on the autumn-tinted Cumberland Plateau.

Below: Horses graze in Cades Cove, known for its trail-riding. The state's reputation for excellent horse breeding dates back to the days of Andrew Jackson, when the best stallions and mares were imported from the eastern United States and Europe.

Right: This young ocelot is among many species of wild cats residing at the Memphis Zoo's Cat Country exhibit. The zoo's other extensive outdoor exhibits include Penguin Rock, where black-footed penguins native to southern and southwestern Africa adjust perfectly to the hot Memphis summer.

Far right: The three-acre China Exhibit at the Memphis Zoo reproduces the country's buildings, plant life, and even sounds, and provides a home for giant pandas, hog deer and Asian small-clawed otters.

Below: A giant panda readies for a nap in its home at the Memphis Zoo.

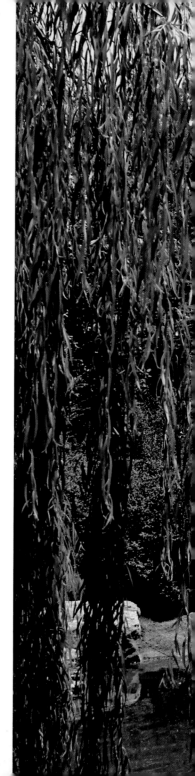

Left: A clear day on the Big South Fork Cumberland River in northern Tennessee. The Big South Fork National River and Recreation Area protects the river and its tributaries, along with miles of scenic gorges and sandstone bluffs.

Below, left: A mimosa, or silk tree, finds a roadside spot in Clarksville. A popular ornamental originally introduced in 1745, the mimosa now grows in areas ranging from New Jersey to Louisiana.

Below, middle: Covering thousands of acres, nine species of native shrubs in the rhododendron genus live in Great Smoky Mountains National Park.

Below, right: Echinacea, or purple coneflower, is one of the most popular and widely used herbs in American and European herbal medicine.

Left: Fireside at a Civil War reenactment of the Battle of Franklin, which was fought on November 30, 1864, in central Tennessee.

Far left: Fort Loudoun State Park near Vonore commemorates the site of one of the earliest British fortifications on the western colonial frontier. Living history displays include artillery and musket drills similar to those of the 1750s.

Below: A blacksmith toils at Mansker's Station, which is an authentic reconstruction of a 1779 frontier fort in the Cumberlands near Goodlettsville.

Right: Vessels of many sizes ply the mighty Mississippi River as it flows through western Tennessee to Memphis and beyond.

Below: Horses silhouetted at sunset. Tennessee is the only state to lend its name to one of the world's most popular horse breeds, the Tennessee Walking Horse. Introduced in 1939, Shelbyville's annual Tennessee Walking Horse National Celebration attracts horse owners from across the United States.

Left: Trillium's gentle hues brighten early spring.

Far left: New growth surfaces at a tobacco farm on the Cumberland Plateau. Tobacco's yield of dollars per acre prompts researchers to look for ways to utilize in foods and medicine, its beneficial ingredients, such as vitamins, beta carotene, and amino acids, in foods and medicine.

Below: Early spring wildflowers are sheltered beneath a log.

Above: Built from the Lorraine Motel, the site of Martin Luther King's assassination in 1968, the National Civil Rights Museum in downtown Memphis is the nation's first comprehensive exhibit chronicling America's civil rights movement.

Right: The Main Street Trolley in Memphis is part of the city's Heritage Trolley system. The Main Street and Riverfront route parallels the Mississippi River and features cars with varnished interior woodwork and the classic lines of 1900-era trolleys.

Left: Built in 1999, the Women's Basketball Hall of Fame in Knoxville covers 100-plus years of national women's basketball by honoring the sport's past, celebrating its present, and promoting its future. Numerous cities and towns across Tennessee have contributed championship women players to schools and teams across the United States.

Far left: A modern frontiersman carrying the University of Tennessee flag urges diehard fans to cheer on the football team. UT's sports teams, the Volunteers, or "Vols," are named for the Tennessee soldiers who volunteered to fight in the War of 1812. REPRINTED WITH PERMISSION FROM THE UNIVERSITY OF TENNESSEE HEALTH SCIENCE CENTER.

Left: Wildflowers line the Appalachian National Scenic Trail as it traverses Great Smoky Mountains National Park. The trail runs 2,175 miles through 14 states from Maine to Georgia. These wildflowers are included among the 1,660 types of blooming plants found within the park's boundaries, more than in any other national park in North America.

Facing page: Jack Daniel's own likeness graces the entrance to Cave Spring, source of the limestone spring water used at his famed whiskey distillery founded in Lynchburg in 1866. Despite the distillery, Moore County, the smallest county in Tennessee, remains a "dry" county.

Left: The view from Point Park on the top of historic Lookout Mountain overlooks the Tennessee River's Moccasin Bend and the city of Chattanooga. The point is one of the historic sites at Chickamauga and Chattanooga National Military Park, established by Congress to honor the memory of the battles in 1863 between Union and Confederate forces for control of Chattanooga.

Below, left: The Gordon House and Ferry site is located west of Columbia on the Natchez Trace Parkway. Ferry operations across the Duck River began in 1801 and continued for more than ninety years. The house, built for the Captain John Gordon, the ferry operator, and his family, dates from 1818. The Natchez Trace Parkway follows 444 miles of trails established by game, and later traveled by Native Americans and early farmers from the Mississippi River through Alabama to central Tennessee.

Below, right: The Alex Haley House and Museum in Henning is the final resting place of the award-winning writer. Haley's novel *Roots*, which traced his ancestry back to Africa, was translated into more than thirty languages and was made into a successful television mini-series. The 10-room house, built in 1919 by Haley's maternal grandparents, was his boyhood home for several summers. On its front porch, Haley first heard the stories of Kunta Kinte, his young Mandingo ancestor from West Africa.

Right: Immortalized in song by band leader Glenn Miller, the Chattanooga Choo Choo comes to life at the Southern Railway Terminal in downtown Chattanooga. The architecturally imposing terminal was renovated in the 1970s into a hotel with accompanying shops and railway-related attractions.

Far right: As dusk falls on the Parkway, a ribbon of lights stretches from Pigeon Forge all the way back through Sevierville.

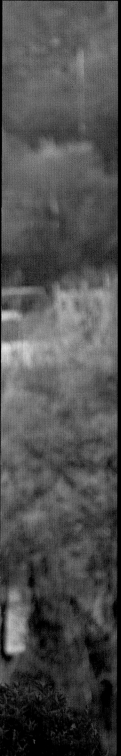

Left: The Port Royal Covered Bridge settles into winter as it spans the Red River in Port Royal State Park near Adams, in north-central Tennessee. A replica of the original bridge that washed away in the 1860s, the covered bridge has twice been rebuilt following storms.

Far left: Bluffs above the Tennessee River beckon art lovers outdoors at the River Gallery Sculpture Garden in downtown Chattanooga's Bluff View Art District. Historic homes and working art studios share the district with the Hunter Museum of American Art, the Houston Museum of Decorative Arts, as well as cafes and gardens. The neighborhood was designed in the nineteenth century to resemble a small European village, which is reflected in the area's landscaping and architecture.

Right: Specks of light emerge as the sun sets on Center Hill Lake in the Cumberland Mountains of middle Tennessee. The lake's 415 miles of shoreline, managed by the U.S. Army Corps of Engineers, remain largely undeveloped and natural.

Below: The Foothills Parkway originates near Townsend and skirts the northern edges of Great Smoky Mountains National Park. The wispy, smoke-like fog that gives the Smoky Mountains their name results from rain, and evaporation from trees. Upper elevations receive as much as 85 inches of rain per year.

Above: The "Skyscraper" is one of the many hands-on interactive exhibits at the Children's Museum of Memphis.

Left: The Clyde Parke Miniature Circus, circa 1930, is one of the chief attractions at the Pink Palace Museum in Memphis. A 1-inch to 1-foot scale model of a traveling circus, it features a 15-foot canvas Big Top, hand-carved mechanized acrobats and horses, and a motorized grand entry parade. Its creator, Clyde Parke, saw his first circus at the age of eight. He began carving the model during the Great Depression for "children of all ages."

Right: The Chucalissa Museum and Archaeological Site, operated by the University of Memphis, includes a reconstructed American Indian village that portrays life in the Mississippi valley from AD 1000 to 1500. Archaeological digs began here after the accidental discovery of a Mississippian mound complex in the 1930s.

Far right: The bedroom of legendary railroad engineer Casey Jones is on display at his restored 1890s family home at Casey Jones Village in Jackson.

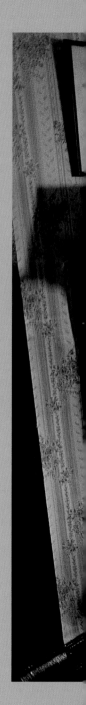

Cornmeal is milled six days a week at the Old Mill and General Store on the Little Pigeon River in Pigeon Forge. Until 1935, the Old Mill and its water wheel

Making a broom at an Appalachian crafts demonstration in Pigeon Forge.

Voodoo supplies for sale at A. Schwab Dry Goods, on Beale Street in Memphis. In business since 1876, the store still carries an assortment of other wares, including clothes and kitchen supplies. It is considered one of the city's historic treasures.

Right: Installed in his hometown of Nashville, a statue of Andrew Jackson, one of three U.S. presidents from Tennessee, stands before legislators and citizens at the Tennessee State Capitol.

Far right: Architectural details abound on this Memphis courthouse.

Left: Broad and beautiful, these waterfalls of the Middle Prong Little River greet hikers along the Middle Prong Trail in Great Smoky Mountains National Park. Not far away at Tremont, the Great Smoky Mountains Institute offers environmental education for all ages in a residential setting.

Below: Abrams Falls, on Abrams Creek in Great Smoky Mountains National Park, is only 20 feet high, but the rush of water belies its lack of height. The cascade ends peacefully in a long, deep pool at its base. The stream is named for a Cherokee Chief Abram or Abraham, whose village once stood several miles downstream

Right: An entertainment district since the 1920s, Beale Street retains its reputation as the home of the blues and the birthplace of rock 'n roll. Here the music of the blues was first written down, and performed nightly in the clubs and venues that welcomed it up from the Mississippi Delta.

Below: The legendary Sun Records Recording Studio in Memphis lit up the careers of Elvis Presley, Jerry Lee Lewis, B. B. King, Roy Orbison, and many others.

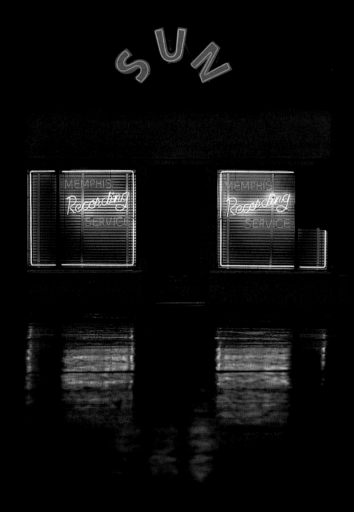

Left: A sculpture of baseball players plays eternally in front of the Hunter Museum of American Art, in downtown Chattanooga's Bluff View Art District. The centerpiece of a revitalized neighborhood, the museum is housed in a 1904 Classical Revival mansion and exhibits American art ranging from the Hudson River School to abstract expressionism.

Far left: This talented skateboarder is featured among the numerous pieces of outdoor sculpture on display in downtown Chattanooga's Bluff View Art District.

Right: The 266-foot Sunsphere, with observation decks and five levels of reflective bronze-coated glass windows, continues to be the centerpiece of World's Fair Park in Knoxville. A water park, spacious lawns, shops, and an amphitheatre are among the park's many features incorporated from the site's 1982 World's Fair.

Far right: The Great Smoky Mountains, as seen from the observation tower on the summit of Clingmans Dome. At 6,643 feet, Clingmans Dome is the highest point in Great Smoky Mountains National Park, and the highest point in Tennessee. The biological diversity found in the park, from large mammals to microscopic organisms, is the greatest of any temperate climate zone in the world.

Left: The Old Mill, on the Little Pigeon River in Pigeon Forge. Established in the early 1800s and now listed in the National Register of Historic Places, it is one of the most photographed mills in the United States.

Far left: A young visitor removes her shoes for a visit to Mud Island River Park in Memphis. The park's River Walk is a 5-block-long replica of the lower Mississippi River, with each 30 inches representing one mile along the river from Cairo, Illinois to New Orleans, Louisiana. Historic events and geographic transformations are noted along the way.

Right: Kayakers paddle downriver near The Narrows, on the Harpeth River in middle Tennessee. Harpeth River State Park parallels the river and includes hiking trails, along with canoeing and kayaking access points.

Below: Visitors to Dollywood cool off at Splash Country, adjacent to the main theme park in Pigeon Forge. Entertainer Dolly Parton developed the 125-acre park in the foothills of the Smoky Mountains to showcase Appalachian culture, music, and traditional crafts. The park's dozen-plus musical stage shows include mountain, bluegrass, and gospel acts.

Above: An aerial view of farmland in central Tennessee's Rutherford County. The county's many productive farms benefit from a moderate climate, long growing season, and ready access to markets. Farms held by the same family for at least one hundred years are certified as Century Farms.

Left: Trees shelter Sevierville. Romantic spots in the Great Smoky Mountains are popular wedding sites. According to the local chamber, Sevier County is second only to Las Vegas for the number of marriages performed there.

BOB SCHATZ

Bob Schatz's admiration of photography began as a small child. Before he was six, his parents discovered that he had been sneaking his father's camera, and a neighbor came to the rescue with a gift of a Brownie box camera for Schatz's birthday by the age of eight. Self-taught throughout his childhood and adolescence, he went on to Belmont University, where he entered a couple of prints in a statewide photography competition his sophomore year. Although he lost first place to a professor at another college, Schatz was eager to pursue his passion throughout his college years. He won 'Best in Show' at the Nashville Art Directors Guild by his senior year. His photographs continue to be recognized, winning many regional and national awards.

PHOTO BY RALPH ZWICKER

Schatz's craft has a proven track record of over thirty years, and his work is frequently seen in print and internet advertising, corporate brochures, annual reports, books, and magazines. His clientele includes *Time* magazine, Honeywell International, and many others. His artworks have been exhibited around the country and are included in the permanent collections of museums, corporations, and private collectors. Schatz's portfolio can be viewed at www.stockschatz.com, and his blog is at www.bobschatz.com.